Tribute Poems
from
the Malvern Spoken Word Group
Edited by Jane Winter and Francis Charters

What is a 'tribute poem'?

To be honest we made up the term during one of our spoken word meetings in Malvern, Worcestershire. One of us had just read out a rewrite of a famous poem and, after some discussion, we realised that others had either written new versions of poems or verse inspired by other poets' work.

That was when we came up with the term 'tribute poem'.

Some idiot (*that would be me*) then suggested that we should collate a book of tributes in tribute to the originals and in celebration of new verse.

This is the volume you are now reading.

Francis Charters
www.malvernspokenword.blogspot.com

Contents

1 Forgetfulness
A tribute to the poem 'Forgetfulness' by Billy Collins

The name should be the first to go
followed by the title, you have lost the plot,
the catastrophic conclusion is not novel,
becomes one told time in time, known and heard of,

as if, memories you don't want to harbour
decide to stay and retreat to parts of the brain,
to a tiny hamlet where there are no phones.

Long ago I slammed the door without goodbye
and watched the taxi driver load my bag,
the moon was pinioned amongst the planets,

I slipped away, a wraith in the darkness perhaps,
to the place of an old friend, not as far away as Paraguay,

a friend you struggle to yet fail to remember,
because you never bothered to have it on the tip of your tongue
or anywhere else, let alone in the darkness of your spleen.

I floated away to the sea via a radiant river
whose name is Sabrina as I happily recall

well on my way to a life without you I shall join those
who have never forgotten how to ride a bicycle.

No wonder you wake in your woebegone night
to regret your spite, our battles, our war.
No wonder to you the moon is just an orb that drifted
out of a love poem that you never knew by heart.

By Polly Stretton ©

2 To my grandfather

A tribute to the poem 'Do not go gentle into that good night' by Dylan Thomas

Go, Go gentle into that good night.
Do not fight that final leaving,
Still believing in a better place
Than this.

Go, go, leave the simple heart beat
And complete your aged restoration,
Full salvation, free of
Body parts.

Go and leave those faulty body parts
That break the hearts of those who knew
You through a life of
Wit and strength.

Go now, safely on your heavenly way
And let today bring true relief
And peace to all
Who love you.

By Francis Charters ©

3 Not Quaffing but Coughing
A tribute to the poem 'Not waving but drowning' by Stevie Smith

everyone heard him, at the back of the hall
quite still: he lay gurgling;
we thought he was drunk and that was his call
but he was coughing not quaffing.

Poor chap, he always loved barking
and now he lies like a lump of lead;
a timely Heimlich manoeuvre might have saved him,
they said.

Oh, no no no, it was not his usual call
(the inebriate's gurning)
he drank far too much all his life
and he was coughing not quaffing.

By Stephen Chappell ©

4 Garage August 2024
A tribute to the poem 'The Lady of Shalott' by Alfred Lord Tennyson

I'd booked the work well in advance,
Hoping my car's health to enhance.
As I walked in they looked askance,
Then gave me a much kinder glance,
The local car mechanics.
'Yes love?' they asked me through the gloom,
Breathing a mix of diesel fume,
Exhaust and oil - a man's perfume -
A heady, hopeful mix.

Pinned to the peeling grimy walls,
The bright adverts laid out their stalls:
They claimed success with no pitfalls.
A man smiles in his overalls -
The local car mechanics.
Certificates claim membership -
Professional - and craftsmanship,
Skill and patience and workmanship -
A heady hopeful mix.

I sit, wait in the grimy room.
I peer around and through the gloom.
They'll fix my car, I must assume;
They would not leave me to my doom,
The local car mechanics.
The oil can, 'Castrol' writ in red,
Stained worn black matting - not a thread.
Large green oil drum across the shed:
A heady hopeful mix.

The children's books stuffed in the rack,
Beside a table with a stack
Of magazines with lifestyle hacks
In this rusted iron shack.
The local car mechanics

Suggest I need a pricey part
To fix my car and make it start.
Their confidence does trust impart -
A heady hopeful mix.

So finally the engine fires,
Horn blares, mechanic waves his pliers.
He checks the oil, and kicks the tyres,
Confirms that there are no loose wires,
The local car mechanics.
My visit to the service station
(Of appreciable duration)
Has given rise to adulation -
A heady, hopeful mix.

By Jane Winter ©

5 Valediction
A tribute to John Keats

Wracked by pain ... coughing blood, in the warmth of Italy:
Don't weep dearest Fanny,
For I have walked the fields of Autumn,
Heard nightingales singing far above,
Gathered flowers, gifts of love ...
Wreaths for the dead.
Brilliance too soon ... flew near the sun.
Burnt out before life had? begun,
I cough my heart out in the sun.
If I had but time enough to tell.
'Hear the bell toll.' My death knell.

Glorious days when you were mine,
Red ring on your finger, joy sublime.
Scarlet my pillow, with life's blood,
My heart aches for your smile, dear sweet love ...
Dream of those days when life was mine,
Time to roam in the countryside.
Tom, my brother, still alive,
Future love, you by my side.
I am dying in Italy in the sun,
True friend by my bed,
Life's journey run.
Colour red, the dying sun.

I dream of the soft grass under foot,
The joy of friendship, a poetry book,
Long conversations under trees,
Soft stirring zephyrs, gentle breeze.
Enduring friendship, like minded souls,
Dear poets and artists, your hand to hold ...
Do not forget me, mourn for a while,

My lips kiss your fingers, dear sweet child.
My name writ in water, still, cool, running free;
My Life blood red ... crimson. Death in Italy.
☐

As one with the Autumn, leaves turn to gold, scarlet, brown,
Drift softly down, return to the earth, life's circle run.
I die in the sun ...
Have been so blessed, found love and friendship through poesy.
The urge to write has lifted me,
Soaring free, beyond the stars to ecstasy:
At one with all eternity, not dying here in Italy.

Weep not for me. For I have journeyed with Homer and Euripides
...
Found inspiration in the sun - Endymion
Soared singing with the nightingale.
The poetry of earth is never dead ...
Not here in bed ... pillow red ...
I walk through fields of golden corn, sun kissed cheeks,
Arms full of flowers.
Long blissful hours, this world is ours ...
"Shed no tear - O shed no tear."
I am the sun touching your cheek,
The gentle breeze lifting your hair.
As true loves lives, I will be there.

By Jean Parrott ©

6 Love

A tribute to the poem 'The Silent Articulation of a Face' by Rumi

Because you're centred in love
love can find you and encircle you
Because you speak gently
softness pads your heart
Because your heart has filters fine as silver thread
only pure light can enter
Because the commerce of your heart is kindness
the universe will open its storehouse to you
Trust in love
Love and trust.

By Rushna ©

7 Making Cocoa for Wendy Cope

Who'd dream
of rustling up a Horlicks
or some Ovaltine
for Kingsley Amis now
not someone to whom to kow tow
anymore
not now.

Misogynist git -
though I must admit
Lucky Jim
made me larf a bit;

but Wendy's stolen his mantle
no shit
and let it be known:
it was the dream she had was vital

she says she only wrote it down
because of the brilliant title.

And now I've done the same.
Oh, the shame!
Blimey!
What fun we can have
with a famous name...

By Stephen Chappell ©

8 Voices from the Park

A tribute to the poem 'The hunchback in the park' by Dylan Thomas

Each slate green day
Chapel fresh
Haddock eyes wide with longing
The tide washes me in
Like bleached flotsam
Its single ebb
A turgid wave whose salty embrace
Erases life's disappointments.

Each day the call
Reaches me
Even when the sky is dull
And solemn sleet-filled rain
Keeps gulls silent
And men in boats
Forsake the greedy ocean's swell
Cursing from cobbled cottages.

Piercing as truth
Sleep robbing
The park's dark whisper beckons
And my mind's eye drifts
Rushing onwards
Through opened gates
To the municipal water,
Over regulated grass.

No dreams for me
Of dainty parks
With gently lapping crimson waves
Sparkling with gaudy golds
Its garish colours
Luscious as peaches
Over exciting the senses
Like mermaids in Swansea Bay.

The greatest skill
Is to craft
With a harsh muted palette
Borders whose safe edges
Are straight as a chapel pew
As unyielding as a Sabbath sermon.
I'm called to curb
Fallen leaves
Cheery chattering matrons
And uninvited vagrants
Whose ragged untidiness
Invites devilment in mocking urchins

And as tides turn
I thrust back
The detritus of the day
Watching it float away
The boys that swarm
Round the tramp
And the over curious idlers
Cast out by the park for their irreverence.

By Jeremy Harwood ©

9 Gin is Free

A tribute to the poem 'The Lake Isle of Innisfree' by W B Yeats

I shall alight and go now to where the gin is free
And a tall noggin buy there of glass and bottles made
Nine beer towers will I have there and a dive for the money beans
And live alone in a booze-cowed glaze.

And I shall have some ease there for ease comes dropping slow
Dropping from the scale of gulping to how each gullet sings,
Where midnight's just gone numb-er, and noon's a boozy glow
And evening's full of cock-tailed stings.

I will arise and go now, for always night and day
I hear the whisky tapping with low sounds on my door
While I slump on the roadway, or on the pavement grey
I feel it in the steep hung o'er!

By Phil Dahl ©

10 Late
A tribute to the poem 'The Air Year' by Caroline Bird

Your thoughts are clouds thrown across an otherwise empty sky,
Like milk dropped in a hugeness of tea, or the spreading stain
Of blood in a bath, and although you try to make them move
A little quicker there is no other way for you to span this blue divide -
At least that's what you think, for in this insubstantial after-state its hard
To do things any way at all.
                            You let your hands fall through the desk
And leave your head to do the same a moment later, whilst in the dark
Street below your open window the dogs are calling out your name.
The only thoughts condensing now are: should you answer them, and
how?

The rest remains unrealised water.

By Martin Worster ©

11 Hidden door
A tribute to Robert Frost

This hidden door is lost to view
Only glimpsed if someone knew
Where to look or what to see
Beyond that creeping ivy tree.

Barely noticed passing by,
Little catches any eye;
But this pensive random look
Catches how it shapes the nook.

Where it leads we might suspect
From such witness to neglect -
Just forgotten, left to rot.
Should it open up or not?

What conceals could just divert,
Steal our sight from what's covert:
Stories someone wants to block;
Secrets yet to be unlocked.

Who'd now dare to snap that lock,
Wind again its time-trapped clock?
In such closures we might find
Nightmares best left out of mind.

By Phil Dahl ©

12 The Dustmen
A tribute to the poem 'The Hollow Men' by TS Elliot

What are those shadows
in the early dawn?
Those fish-fisted figures
calling through the mist?
I can only remember my name
Oh that I should I remember it now!
so far from Ocle Pychard

Stab egg with knife!
Stab egg with knife!
There is no mystery here
only the wind in Westfaling Street
and the dry chuckle of the fading train
"She'll be coming round the mountain
when she comes..." Yes.
But why!?
Who? And, for Heaven's sake,
when!?

You danced behind the abandoned nunnery
in the thickening snow
with more snow falling
We smoked long thin begonias then
and wore pink pyjamas

Oh, what is the point of it all!

There are only blind witnesses
here, at the accident

There
where time builds
beaks and fingers
in its magical multicoloured casings
you read me runny in the Book of Eggs

24

and woke me
in a folding bed
with instructions from the brainless dead
who sang in the bag of burning heads
you dug up from an ocean
where the maniac
wipes haddock from his trousers

In time
I too
would teach you how to move
and where.

I'd teach you time...
where Time is...
was...
Oh!
I could go on and on
and on
(we all could)
generating clouds of Mercutio's 'Blah, blah!'
in the muddled babble
(as the rabble
will have it)
or the bottled-up
garble
(as the troubled
gabble it)
from the agonising struggle
where the rubble jams it
to the sheer relief
as the bubbles exit
Pop!
Pop!
Pop!
go the dustmen.

By Mo Murrie ©

13 Ozymandias 2024

A tribute to the poem 'Ozymandias' by Percy Bysshe Shelley

I met a journalist from Channel 4
Who said – 'Five loud and feckless Tory men
And women have this country stood before...
Prime Ministers, all promising and then
Austerity, pandemic, and yet more
Caused chaos, misery, utter distress
Through rank corruption and mismanagement.
While scrutiny they all sought to suppress.'
And on the sliding banner did appear:
'The title is Mother of all Parliaments!
Look at her scrutinise you - may you fear
The Ruin of Reputation and Respect -
The cries of citizens you did not hear
As faith in politicians you have wrecked.'

By Jane Winter ©

14 Terminus
A tribute to the poem 'The Whitsun Weddings' by Philip Larkin

And as the train at last begins to slow,
To start with almost imperceptibly,
The sharper focussed vista starts to show
The backs of houses, constant though they seem -
Each one defined by details flashing by.
Untended grass and random piles of scrap,
Or tidy veg plots in their ordered rows.
Caged trampolines pick out a family,
Sun loungers speak of library books and naps.
But as the sense of the familiar grows

You start to see the yellow marker posts
Showing the miles to the finish line;
The numbers flash, ethereal as ghosts -
Glimpsed for a second and then redefined
By something lower. You cannot reverse
This flow of time and distance. It dictates
The ticking of the metronome that cues
All of our unique journeys to converge
Upon the altar preordained by fate,
Lingering up the line, just out of view.

Too soon we will arrive at our final
Destination. Yes, this applies to you.
We are emerging from the last tunnel
Blinking at low sun and the evening dew.
Across the points, the long slow final bend,
Look how the sleek steel rails lead the way
Into the overarching glass train shed,
The journey's fixed, uncompromising end.
Drop from the train, into the last of days.
Joining the almost living - nearly dead.

Step on the slope into the grey ravine,
The escalator drifts like marshland mist
Through custom halls; will someone intervene
To say "It's not your time, you still exist"?
Almost as if in an hypnotic trance
Your mouth is open but emits no sound.
You cannot say that there's been some mistake,
There's no escaping this macabre dance.
Continue down into the underground
And board the train with just one stop to make.

By Peter Clark ©

15 Stooping by boots on a snowy evening
A tribute to 'Stopping by Woods on a Snowy Evening' by Robert Frost

Whose boots these are I cannot know,
abandoned here, half-filled with snow,
a sight so rare, surpassing queer.
Where was he from? Where did he go

on such an evening, chill and drear?
Perhaps he's dead and somewhere near,
hanged in the woods, drowned in the lake.
Scaring myself, I prick an ear,

listen for sounds his ghost might make,
mourning his life, dead yet awake;
half hear his stealthy barefoot creep
and cross myself for pity's sake.

These woods are lonely, dark and deep.
The dread dead wretch, I hear him weep –
I must away, I dare not sleep!
I must away, I dare not sleep!

Derek Healy November 2024 ©

16 Coward

A tribute to the poem 'Young Fellow My Lad' by Robert Service

"The post this morning, young fellow my lad,
Had a letter for you, I hear?"
"Twas a letter to go and join up Dad,
But I can't join up, 'cos I fear
The letter that goes to make people sad
Saying that their son is dead.
That letter would drive right through me, Dad
When I'm asleep in my bed."

"So you're an objector, a coward, my lad,
You're scared of the blood and the weather.
You're scared of the pain, if shot up bad,
And blind to the telling white feather.
Go out there and fight, I think it's odd
You shouldn't be one of the crowd.
Go out there for me, go out there for God,
Just join up and make your Dad proud.

So there was my father, breadwinner, Dad,
Looking despising at me.
The last time I saw him was that time so sad,
He was dead by the time I was free.
Three years behind bars, and God how I thought,
Of decision, if good or if bad.
Of people who died, of people who fought,
        Of life,
                        and of death,
                                        and of Dad.

By Francis Charters ©

17 Walkies
A tribute to the poem 'Daffodils' by William Wordsworth

I wandered lively as a dog,
Snuffling and eager through the mud,
A leg cocked here, poo over there ...
Grey skies above, but do I care?
What bliss it is to be alive,
Snuffling along, you by my side.
Eager to please in your quaint way:
Dead rabbit too, oh blissful day!
A welcome roll I'll take in that,
Clean me later if you must ...
Time to go! Oh heavenly day ...
What joy it is to live this way!

By Jean Parrott ©

18 Kitty

A tribute to the poem 'The Owl and the Pussy-Cat' by Edward Lear

The owl and kitty were all at sea
for kitty had missed a month,
they had no money, and now his honey
was going to make them three.
The Owl picked up his small guitar
and prayed to the stars above,
I beg you, this cannot be true,
how could I be such a fool!
A fool,
A fool,
How could I be such a fool!

Kitty said to the owl, 'What will we do now
you've ruined my reputation?'
It's time we were married,
too long we have tarried,
whilst you just strum and sing!
The Owl who was an honourable fowl,
who dreamed of being a musician.
He said to Kitty,
'Oh Kitty my love,
my lovely Kitty, I will make it good.
But where will we find a ring?'
They sailed away, and eventually came
to an island of coconut groves
where they found a Pig
who was playing a jig
with rings on ends of his toes,
his toes,
his toes,
with rings on the ends of his toes.

Pig was willing to give them two rings and after a brief discussion
they decided to stay and were wed next day
by a turkey who played percussion.
After the wedding feast, Pig played a jig,
Kitty sang and the others joined in.
That night they danced on the edge of the sand
and by the light of the moon they formed a band,
A band,
A band,
By the light of the moon they formed a band,
and now they're YouTube stars.

By Io Osborn   ©

19 When Mother was bathing her baby

An extension in tribute to the traditional music hall song of the same name.

Traditional words

A muvver was bathing her biby one night
The youngest of ten, and a tiny wee mite.
The muvver was poor and the biby was thin
Only a skelington covered wiv skin
The muvver turned round for the soap orf the rack
She weren't but a moment, but when she turned back
Her biby was gawn and in anguish she cried
'Oh where is my biby?' The Angels replied,

Chorus:
'Your baby has gone down the plug-hole
Your baby has gone down the plug
The poor little thing was so skinny and thin
It should have been washed in a jug
Your baby is ever so happy
He won't need a bath any more
Your baby has gone down the plughole
Not lost but gone before.'

Extension verses

The muvver she really was angry.
"You've no right to 'ave 'im" said she,
"Now take me to see that St Peter,
Or I'll 'ave you over me knee!"
The Angels did as they were bidden
And at the gates pearly she stood.
An old man with flowing white beard
Asked her if she'd been very good:

Continued...

"I suppose that you are that there Saint Peter?
I've not come about me" she cried –
"I was bathing my bibe in the baisin last night
And your angels tell me that he's died!"
She shook her fist hard at St Peter,
The old man, he backed off in fear,
"Now don't be so wild, here is your child,
Take him and go home, my dear!"

'Your baby he went down the plughole,
 So next time, just put in the plug –
We don't want him here for many a year,
He'll probably grow up a thug!'

By Jan Scrine ©

20 The Church

A tribute to the poem 'Hiawatha' by H W Longfellow

Walking in a country churchyard
A bearded biker felt a presence
Soft below the monkey puzzle
Felt a gentle Godly presence.

"Are you there God?" asked the sinner
"In the stature of this building?
In rejuvenated lighting?
In the money and the pictures?
In the bureaucratic mountain?
Are you there God?"

"No" he answered, "No, I'm not there
In the heap of antique brickwork,
In the paintings and the guilt-ware,
In the Sunday church attendance
And long words and lusty singing.

But you'll see me, you will find me
In the hearts of all my children
In their prayers and their vocation,
In every touch and every kindness
That they pay to weak and weary.
Honest praise and adulation
Shows my power and shows my presence.
Even in a humble stable
With no stately arched stained windows
With no organ costing thousands
With no law that's made for Sunday's
You may find a baby crying
For the blindness of my children,
For the sins that have been paid for."
Then the greying bearded sinner
Asked his God another question,
Another plea to the Almighty.

"Should I leave the village parish?
Should I go to pastures yonder?
Pray to you alone in silence,
Like a monk, a vow of silence?"

"No" said God, our great Almighty,
"Do not leave your church in Malvern
Do not take a vow of silence.
But pray simply, pray so deeply
For a leader of your parish
Who will know the truth of my word
Who will know a love so Godly
Comes from prayer and heartfelt feeling
Not from rules and bricks and mortar
Not from earthly institutions."

Saying this the vision vanished
And the man with joy went forward,
Up the hill towards his soul base
Where he greeted friends and family
Greeted them with words of wisdom
Joining them in prayer devoted
To arrival of a vicar
Who could lead our small church forward
In the love of our Almighty.

By Francis Charters ©

24 The spider and the sundial
Imagist D. H. Lawrence tribute

Casting no shadow, the fine-spun threads hug and cling
to the reaching rusty arm angling the old sky,
a finger pointing to a new sun.
No hands but marks inscribe the edge
which might just show or tell the time,
whenever light shapes into shades,
as ancient as shadows.

It's just as hard to tell where she is, the maker
of the web: this weaver of spin. Uncertain patterns
trace fragility across a space of air, the cast of hours:
so skilled at concealment and tricks, her presence -
implied as much as obvious, innately subtle -
reflects a lasting intention of survival.

Perhaps the dawn's dew, maybe the last rain,
globes the web in reflections of lands,
minute, but changing moment by minute,
as the daylight moves, dialling its passing.
The weaver of worlds lends both their form,
to shape and puzzle the space,
turning aeons to instants, mountains
to valleys by ice flows, as breaths
become ages, imagined as streams.

A cloud passes, throwing shadows from distance
to cross that blade, sharp enough to read
and cut angles making shapes between
the spider and the sundial.

by Phil Dahl ©

21 Prayer

A tribute to the song 'Reason for Living' by Francis Rossi and Rick Parfitt

Once, on a cold and clear morning
At the breaking of the day
A blackbird, it was calling
And the song thrush had it say
I sat in silence on my seat
And said a simple prayer
And waited for an answer sweet
But nobody was there.

I'd heard that God was all around
Not in a church of stone.
But there I heard no Godly sound
I sat still all alone.
I listened to the dawning day
That came about through care.
And I listened for an answer
As I said another prayer.

And from the beauty of the day
I heard a gentle voice
That helped me on my stumbling way
And made me make my choice.
Respect and love will see you through
Avoiding every snare.
And remember God's with you
So offer up a prayer.

22 Eve of Stagness

A tribute to the poem 'The Eve of St. Agnes by John Keats

STAGNESS — rough-hewn from a western isle's
farthermost reach, lashed by Atlantic gale
and neighbourless for twenty bleakened miles
of tortured gorse, condemned to writhe and flail
wind-dried arthritic fingers at the wail
of hooded gulls. Stagness — where wreckers plied
their ill-starred trade, where echoes tell the tale
of broken ships, drowned ghosts, of men who died,
throats cut by fiends who lured and pulled them from the tide.

Here in this weary place a castle stands
atop the cliff, though crumbling to the west,
prey to the sea's insatiable demands
for ransom. Lumps of castle are the best!
(A Gothic joke. I hope you're well impressed).
The eastern tower is habitable still
though failing fast the unrelenting test
of time and tempest. Through the cracks the shrill
wind skirls like some demented demon piper's reel.

There in the tower a lonely maiden dwells,
Eve of Stagness, a prisoner by choice
for even when she flips her lid and yells
for help, there's none to hear her silvery voice
(the wind and sea make such a lot of noise).
And how by choice? Alas, she cast her shoes
into the raging sea, which wasn't wise
since twenty miles of gorse is sorry news.
Enthroned alone, she sings her barefoot beauty blues

and eats the fungus that a kindly fate
causes to burgeon, beardlike, from the cracks
around her prison walls. It tastes like late-
bottled chianti laced with carpet tacks
and gingerbread. The only thing she lacks
is human company. "Although I sowed
the seeds of my unhappiness, this smacks
of overkill. Perhaps I'll kiss this toad?"
She did. It turned into a frog and hit the road.

So perished all her plans, until she came
to that abyss that marks the end of flight
from reason, hope and virtue (can you name
another liquidation? Well, all right,
from sanity to boot). She'd lost the fight
and would have yielded to depression's call
but for a dream that came to her by night
when she was sleeping. Must I give you all
the sordid details? She had taken – alcohol...

It seemed to Eve that as she lay asleep
a radiant being appeared beside her bed
proclaiming, "Gee, what funny hours you keep,
it's half past ten. Wake up, you sleepy head
and hear my words. Oh, you can call me Ned".
Startled, she turned. Her covers fell away
and in her lovely nakedness she said
"What bloody man is that?" but Ned was gay
and hadn't time to quote from Shakespeare anyway.

"This very night" he said, "(Oh do keep still,
you make me dizzy when you oscillate)
the lover of your dreams most likely will
attempt to set you free. I shouldn't wait
awake for him, he'll probably be late.
Excuse me now, I've got to disappear".
He did. And Eve was left to contemplate
the meaning of his words. She wasn't clear
if Ned had meant the toad or Wullie from last year.

Another day went by. (The wind and rain
raged as they raged in stanza one, OK?
This epic repetition is a pain
we well can do without.) Another day
of agony for Eve who couldn't say
with anything resembling confidence
if, all in all, she wouldn't rather stay
incarcerated than perhaps commence
imperfect futures with a less than perfect tense

feeling inside. But what will be will be
and Eve succumbed once more to healing sleep,
trusting in Ned because it seemed that he
surely had more to do than tell a heap
of lies, so after counting ninety sheep
she slipped away in line with nature's laws,
cares drifting free like ripples on the deep
for angel promises can show no flaws –
At dawn she wakened in the arms of Santa Claus,

or so he said, and certainly beside
the bed she saw a neatly folded pile
of fur-lined scarlet rags. But when she tried
to picture Christmas cards and reconcile
the beard, the ruddy face and happy smile
with this ill-shaven youth, it wouldn't do.
She said, "Hi Wullie. Here's a fine surprise.
I guess it had to be the toad or you.
Now, rescue me and then we'll have a glass or two".

"What, now?" said Wullie, who had other plans.
"Aye, now!" said Eve, "I've been here long enough,
the food's all gone, I've finished all the cans
and had to live on fungus. It's been tough."
"There's gratitude!" said Wullie. "You can stuff
your castles!" As the cruel words were spoken
a bolt of lightning struck him on the scruff
melting his very bones. Was Eve heartbroken?
Not much. He'd left behind his Reeboks as a token.

By Dave McClure ©

23 Space X

A tribute to Hemingway

Mars beckons, a crimson dream,
Musk's vision, a fiery gleam.
A rocket roars, a silver dart,
A gamble bold, a work of art.
A crew of brave, a chosen few,
Their hearts aflame, their spirits true.
Across the void, they dare to fly,
Beneath a Martian sky.
A dusty plain, a barren land,
A future forged by human hand.
A colony grows, a hope reborn,
A new frontier, a world forlorn.
Yet doubt may linger, a nagging fear,
A cosmic gamble, year after year.
But Musk presses on, unwavering sight,
A dreamer's quest, a noble fight.

By Ian Walker ©

25 The Spoils of War
A tribute to 'The Guns Fell Silent' by Matthew Holloway.

When the guns fell silent we counted up our dead
When the guns fell silent they counted up their dead
So much loss of life, it had to be believed
All the dead accounted, but what had been achieved?

By Tony Cheese ©

26 The Ballad of Sandton Gaol
(written by the pool of the Cullinan Hotel, Johannesburg, May 1998)
A tribute to the poem 'Reading Gaol' by Oscar Wilde

He sat within unbroken walls
and sipped imported beer.
Warm sun played on his shoulders
as he struggled not to hear
the all-pervasive strains that brought
midnight in Vegas near.

And all the inmates round the pool
stretched out and took their ease.
The dowagers drew back their skirts
to tan their leather knees
and who would grudge the simple souls
such simple joys as these?

Around him birds of paradise
flamed with a glorious light.
Palm fronds were still as stalactites
in subterranean night
and all the inmates round the pool,
surprisingly, were white.

Black gaolers walked their sorry pound
among their weary guests.
They carried drinks on trays, and were
immaculately dressed,
their collars, cuffs and trousers all
professionally pressed.

And once a week, lest they be deemed
unreasonably hard,
the gaolers drove their charges to
an exercising yard
where they could stretch the languid rand
and flex the plastic card.

And this the insidious torture of
the exercising mall,
that all the goods were overpriced
and all the portions small,
and not a prisoner was returned
till he had spent his all.

He wandered aimless round the mall
and dreamed of roaming free,
remembered the Pacific coast
and walking in the sea,
and evenings spent in Amsterdam
in joyous company.

He longed to walk the country, as
an unconvicted man.
But there are crimes we can expunge
and those we never can.
His felony - he was not born
into the gaolers' clan.

He thought of things he used to say
before he'd come to face
the pain of a divided land,
where history and race
conspire to speak of all the world
reflected in one place.

By Dave McClure ©

27 Tory Rampage

A tribute to the song 'Teenage Rampage' by Sweet

Boris out.
Boris out.
Boris out.

Across the land, the filthy rich, the lying toffs have got the upper hand.
They ask for thanks for those food banks
They think they are completely in command.

Imagine the sensation of a people's occupation,
A government for the masses
Made of many social classes.
'Cos there's something in the air which we all should be aware.
They don't care! No! No! No! No! No! No!

Come join the revolution
'Gainst governmental prostitution,
Come join the revolution now;
And recognise your age, it's a Tory rampage,
Turn another page on this social outrage.
Now, now, now

They're telling you lies, and they despise
The plebs, but they've got honest eyes.
They're full of hate and they can't wait
To exercise their power.
But this could be our hour.

Imagine the formation of honest legislation
On Brexit they were lying
And in Covid we were dying
'Cos there's something in the air which we all should be aware.
They don't care! No! No! No! No! No! No!

Continued...□

Let's now halt the noise pollution,
Stop the British destitution,
And demand some restitution, now
And recognise your age, it's a Tory rampage
Open up the cage on the current wastage.
Now

Come join the revolution,
Write yourself a constitution,
Let's stop the air pollution, now.
Recognise your age, it's a Tory rampage,
Turn another page on the awful image
Now

Boris out
Boris out
Boris out

28 Dusk sees this sullen sirened city shift
A tribute to the poem 'Fern Hill' by Dylan Thomas

Dusk sees this sullen sirened city shift
Its brisk disguises as my day's face fades
And filters into stage-show shapes and shades
Of twilight. Tween-times cataract my eyes.
My half-moon mind crescents into drift,
The work-glaze surface curdles into blurs.
All space grows thin, my thinking spins and slurs.
Wheel-turned horizons unveil age-free skies.

Day slows: my lulled soul-deafened senses seed
Deep into silence's unease, release
Tombed wounds I'd yearned to spurn, slyly increase
Those life-bound heart's imaginings. I grope
My way as sullied memories stir and bleed
Like echoes catalysing pain-wracked fears.
Such mind-yeast secretly foments the years
Of bodied lives but scopes star-scapes of hope.

Depths seize and scull my city-gryphoned heart
Down into shifting talismanic myths;
Night-glows disguise the mysteries we miss.
We sense beyond each day's keened, dwindling death
A veiled potential as immense a start
As our unwired awareness without poise
Glimpsed once between our silence and our noise,
As intimate as every kindling breath.

Dark sets ghost spells around our shrouded selves
Would cast like concrete each soul's gentling stream
And stun our visioned spirit's untamed dream,
Dungeon our minds to city-limit lines.
A day-down inward memory sparks and delves,
Probes deep, must seek and rescue from the brink
An ageless beckoning sense before we sink
Into that unknown dark where no light shines.

Dawn's breeze then scatters all such dizzy grift
As choruses of sun-bird-song amaze,
Ring out astound the world-turned shape of days
Inspire each darkened sky and eye with sight.
Illusions' shades and wounding echoes lift
as consciousness unchained dispels sour grails;
our dusk-dulled sullen city's mind unveils
a garden that's beyond both dark and light.

By Phil Dahl ©

29 November | Heading for a Country Winter

A tribute to the poem 'Country Summer' by Leonie Adams

In the hedgerows, haws are darkening,
part-abandoned by blackbirds,
they slur to carmine, beyond gems,
beyond melting rubies on the stark bones of May;
they will last over winter until buds return.
The trees are glad of lichen, stark and cold ochre-grey,
no innocence of green remains
and no lark's-bite berries to taste.
The low sun lurks, leers
when it deigns to appear.

Orion the hunter, bright in chill nights,
is easy to recognise
and followed by first frosts in early hours,
tickles of silver and itches of white
where the meadow grass rises, brown yet majestic.
Stray seeds cling and rattle on slender stalks,
defy the onset of the harshest season.
The mowers are in the old barn.
The rust-coated mare is stabled.
Dreams are no longer idle.

By Polly Stretton ©

30 The Traveller

A tribute to the poem 'The Raven' by Edgar Allan Poe

Long ago upon a hilltop (let me finish then I will stop)
I espied a curious traveller where no traveller was before.
As I raised an arm in greeting all at once he took to beating
at the air like one entreating passing boats to come ashore
like a castaway repeating empty movements from the shore
or an over-eager whore.

Never one to wonder blindly I demanded not unkindly
"Are you waving, or behaving in a manner heretofore
generally unexpected, or perhaps you have neglected
to observe the mien affected by humanity before?"
(For he seemed to have elected to gesticulate some more.)
Quoth the traveller "Semaphore".

By Dave McClure ©

31 Larkin About

A tribute to the poem 'This Be The Verse' by Philip Larkin

They fuck you up your politicians
With their lies and stupid admonitions
They may not mean to, but they do
And leave you swimming deep in poo.

But they were fucked up in their turn
By ghastly nitwits from whom they'd learn
To promise cakes to have and eat
And lead you slowly to defeat.

Dire cost of living and high inflation;
Hot rooms with nowt for ventilation,
Climate change and global warming
Have passed them by despite the warning.

They hand on misery to all of us
And for a time we were led by daft Liz Truss
Sometimes I want to have them shot
But I voted in this awful lot.*

*Actually, I didn't. Just put that in to get a rhyme.
No, really, I really didn't. Honest...

By Stephen Chappell ©

32 Sonnet Thirsty

A tribute to sonnet 30 by William Shakespeare

When to the sessions of sweet slumb'rous ales
I summon up remembrance of ales past
I mourn the smack of **Worthingtons** and **Gales**,
Morrells, Morlands, Whitbreads...(p'raps not the last).

Then need I down a glass (well used to flow)
To liquid friends now dry in cheerless night,
To **Eldridge Pope**, to **Woods** (ah, mortal blow!)
To **Tolly Cobbold, Ridleys**, lost from sight;

And grieve for countless others long since gone
Where **Benskins** went, when **Ruddles** shut its door;
Can see no rhyme, just reason put upon
When even bard-like **Brakspears** is no more.

But if the while dear **Donningtons** I drink
All losses are restored, all sorrows sink.

By Derek Healy ©

33 Ledbury

A tribute to the poem 'Adlestrop' by Edward Thomas

Yes. I remember Ledbury—
The name, because one early evening
Of heat the express-train drew up there
Unwontedly. It was late Spring.

There was no one on that bare platform. No staff.
The intercom squawked. Someone cleared their throat.
Due to staffing difficulties, this train will terminate.
Please use the front four carriages only to alight.

Just a smell of hay. The speaker crackled again:
Don't forget your belongings when you alight.
So, we stood under a cloudless sky.
In dismay, all former passengers fell quiet.

One minute on, the platform tannoy blared,
But was drowned out by our train's departure. Silence.
No chirp of swallows. Across Herefordshire,
No birdsong near, nor farther out to the dusky distance.

By Clifford Liles ©

34 The Ploughman

A tribute to the poem 'Daffodils' by William Wordsworth

We clatter loudly like a tank
across the field until the bank
then back again towards the ditch
turning the soil to make it rich
and back towards the bank once more
too many times for keeping score
each second, each minute, each hour
on and on we have to power
on and on, clatter and clatter
preparing for the seeds to scatter
just plodding on unstoppable
to make the ground more arable
ploughing up this classic course
that was for years done by a horse
even so it's still a hard plod
turning every sod and clod
the furrows form a perfect line
while seagulls feast some yards behind
up and down and then repeat
ready for planting this year's wheat
the time I'll never stop to ask
'till after finishing the task
will be done by dusk I'll wager
with my trusty Fordson Major

By Tony Cheese ©

35 Dead Flowers

A tribute to the song 'Dead Flowers' by Mick Jagger and Keith Richards

Well, when you're sitting there in your bald, recycled chair
Talkin' to some down and outs you know
Well, I know you can't see her in that ermined company
Well, you know my best friend's Michelle Mone.

Let me off, little Lady, let me off
I know y'know she made a stash from Boris Toff
And you can ... send her dead flowers every morning
Send her dead flowers by the mail
Send her dead flowers for her peerage
But she won't forget the millions she made.

Well, when you're sitting back in your clapped-out Kodiac
Checking y'card on Lotto Saturday
Ah, She'll be in her Belgrave Home with some Daily Mail buffoon
As another dodgy deal gets underway.

Let me off, little Lady, let me off
I know y'know she spaffed a stash from Boris Toff
And you can - send her dead flowers every morning
Send her dead flowers by the Mail
Send her dead flowers for her peerage,
But she won't forget the millions she made.

Take me down little Lady, take me down
I know y'know her fame's from underwear
And you can - send me damp fag-ends every morning
Send her damp scrag-ends of the (Daily) Mail
Say it with damp fag-ends at her peerage
But she won't forget the millions she made.
No, she won't forget the millions she made.

By Phil Dahl ©

36 The Charge of the Right Brigade

A tribute to the poem 'The Charge of the Light Brigade' by Alfred Lord Tennyson

I
Greens to the Left
Labour to the Right
Into the Election Campaign
  Plunge the six hundred.
"Forward, the Right Brigade!
Lunge for the throat!" Nigel said.
Into the Election Campaign
  Plunge the six hundred.

II
"I'm singing in the Rain!"
Rishi said,
"Look water's pouring on my head
and that awful music –
was it something I said!"

Was there a Tory un-dismayed?
Not though the MPs knew
This fight was Blue on Blue
  Someone had blundered.

But
  Theirs not to make reply,
  Theirs not to reason why,
  Theirs but to do and die.
  Into the valley of Death
  Rode the tory three hundred.

III
Plaid to the West of them,
Scots Nats to the North of them,
Reform, Labour & Lib Dems in front of them
    Who Hooted and Thundered;
Stormed home from Normandy Beaches too soon,
Caught lying about taxes, the damn fool,
Into the jaws of Death,
Into the mouth of hell
    Rode the Tory three hundred.

IV
Flushed all our hard earned cash
down the pan,
Crashed the economy,
Liz Truss the lettuce who ran

Now its just poor Rishi steadying the ship,
Oh what a pity he's such a useless shit

All the world wondered
As Brexit was squandered

Nothing works, the economy is broke;
all they can do is blame the Trans and the Woke
Mortgages sky high!
enough to give you a stroke
We're shattered and sundered.

Post Election they'll be back,
but ALAS & ALACK!
    Not the Tory three hundred.

V
Farage to the right of them,
Starmer to the left of them,
Boris and Braverman behind them
  Volleyed and thundered;

Thatcher's torch has spluttered cold
O the wild lies they told!
  All the world wondered.
Daft the Election they called!
Flat on their bums they sprawled,
  Down down the tubes appalled
The doomed Tory three hundred!

By Stephen Chappell ©

Printed in Great Britain
by Amazon